Christmas Favorites for Harmonica

20 Popular Melodies for Easy Harmonica

Arranged by Eric J. Plahna

T0087806

ISBN 1-4234-0447-5

HAL•LEONARD®
CORPORATION

7777 W. BLUEMOUND RD. P.O. BOX 13819 MILWAUKEE, WI 53213

Visit Hal Leonard Online at
www.halleonard.com

INTRODUCTION

Welcome to *Christmas Favorites for Harmonica*, a collection of 20 holiday songs arranged for easy harmonica. If you're a beginning harmonica player, you've come to the right place; these well-known songs will have you playing and enjoying music in no time! Each melody is presented in an easy-to-read format—including lyrics to help you follow along and chords for optional accompaniment. The harmonica tablature used in this book and discussed on the next page makes playing these Christmas Favorites possible for anyone, even if you don't know how to read music.

As you play through the songs, feel free to choose your own tempo (speed); you can always speed up or slow down according to your ability and preference. Also, try playing some of the melodies with 2 or 3 holes at the same time instead of just one. You'll find that some of the songs sound better this way, while others are more suited to the one-hole approach, or even a mixture of the two.

First, the recommended way to hold your harmonica:

1. Make a "C" with your left hand.
2. Insert the harmonica as shown, holding it firmly but comfortably.
3. Keep your fingers arched slightly. This will allow you to control the sound better.

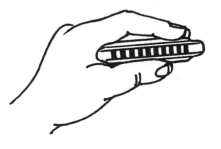

Your right hand should cup, or cradle, your left hand with the fingers coming up around your left hand pinky to form a seal.

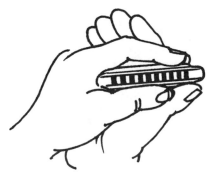

Ultimately of course, you get to choose the most comfortable way to play your harmonica.

HOW TO READ HARMONICA TABLATURE

or

YOU DON'T HAVE TO READ MUSIC TO PLAY THIS BOOK

10-Hole C Diatonic Harmonica

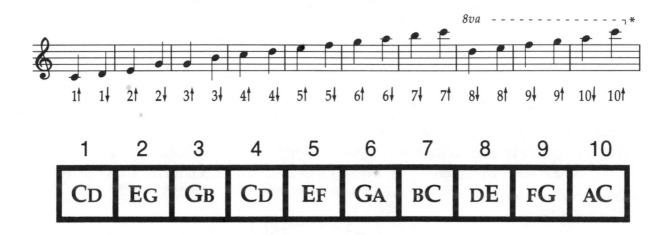

THE BASICS

1. For each note ♩, you are given the number of the hole you are to play.

2. An arrow pointing up ↑ to the right of the number means to **blow** (exhale) that note.

3. An arrow pointing down ↓ to the right of the number means to **draw** (inhale) that note.

Sounds one octave (8 notes) higher than written.

SINGLE NOTES

Single notes can be played in two different ways:

Tongue Blocking

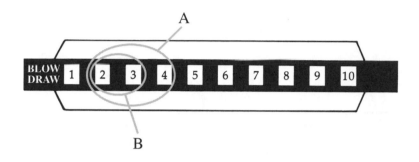

A. Cover three or four notes with your lips, *and...*
B. Cover all the holes with your tongue except the hole on the right

or...

Lipping

1. Pucker your lips so that air passes through one hole.
2. Relax the inside of your mouth, as if you were saying "ah" (very important for good tone).

Again, you may devise a way that is more comfortable for you to achieve a clean single-note sound. There are people who curl their tongue and isolate one tone hole that way.

Blue Christmas

Words and Music by Billy Hayes and Jay Johnson

Caroling, Caroling

Words by Wihla Hutson
Music by Alfred Burt

*Song sounds one octave higher than written.

The Chipmunk Song

Words and Music by Ross Bagdasarian

*Song sounds one octave higher than written.

Feliz Navidad

Music and Lyrics by José Feliciano

*Song sounds one octave higher than written.

Frosty the Snow Man

Words and Music by Steve Nelson and Jack Rollins

*Song sounds one octave higher than written.

Happy Holiday

from the Motion Picture Irving Berlin's "Holiday Inn"

Words and Music by Irving Berlin

*Song sounds one octave higher than written.

I Wonder as I Wander

By John Jacob Niles

1. I won-der as I wan-der out un-der the sky, how Je-sus the
(2.) Ma-ry birth-ed Je-sus, 'twas in a cow's stall, with wise men and

Sav-ior did come for to die for poor or - n'ry peo-ple like you and like
farm-ers and shep-herds and all. But high from God's heav-en a star's light did

I. I won-der as I wan-der out un-der the sky. 2. When
fall, and (the) prom-ise of ___ a - ges it did then re - call. 3. If

Je-sus had want-ed for a - ny wee thing, a star in the

sky or a bird on the wing, or all of God's an-gels in

heav-en to sing, He sure-ly could have had it, 'cause He was the King.

*Song sounds one octave higher than written.

A Holly Jolly Christmas

Music and Lyrics by Johnny Marks

*Song sounds one octave higher than written.

(There's No Place Like)
Home for the Holidays

Words by Al Stillman
Music by Robert Allen

*Song sounds one octave higher than written.

Jingle-Bell Rock

Words and Music by Joe Beal and Jim Boothe

*Song sounds one octave higher than written.

Let It Snow! Let It Snow! Let It Snow!

Words by Sammy Cahn
Music by Jule Styne

Nuttin' for Christmas

Words and Music by Roy Bennett and Sid Tepper

*Song sounds one octave higher than written.

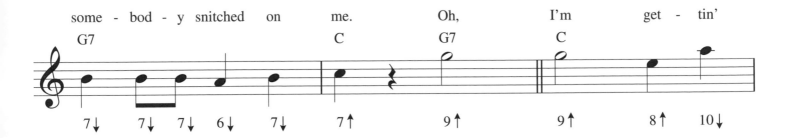

some - bod - y snitched on me. Oh, I'm get - tin'

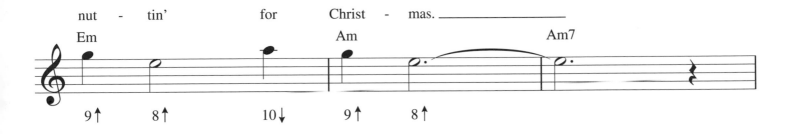

nut - tin' for Christ - mas. _____

Mom - my and Dad - dy are mad. _____

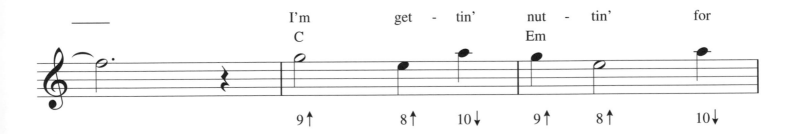

_____ I'm get - tin' nut - tin' for

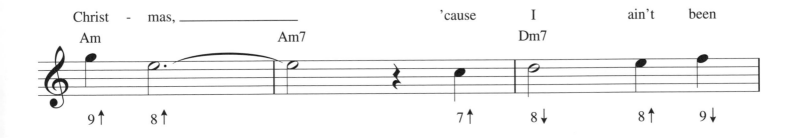

Christ - mas, _____ 'cause I ain't been

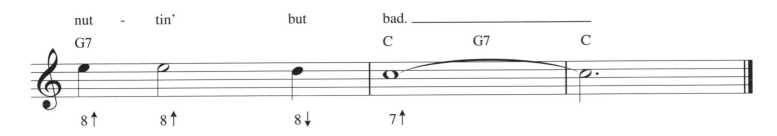

nut - tin' but bad. _____

One for the Little Bitty Baby
(Go Where I Send Thee)

Spiritual Arranged by Ronnie Gilbert, Lee Hays, Fred Hellerman and Pete Seeger

*Song sounds one octave higher than written.

Silver and Gold

Music and Lyrics by Johnny Marks

*Song sounds one octave higher than written.

Rockin' Around the Christmas Tree

Music and Lyrics by Johnny Marks

*Song sounds one octave higher than written.

Rudolph the Red-Nosed Reindeer

Music and Lyrics by Johnny Marks

*Song sounds one octave higher than written.

Santa Claus Is Comin' to Town

Words by Haven Gillespie
Music by J. Fred Coots

*Song sounds one octave higher than written.

Silver Bells

from the Paramount Picture "The Lemon Drop Kid"

Words and Music by Jay Livingston and Ray Evans

*Song sounds one octave higher than written.

Suzy Snowflake

Words and Music by Sid Tepper and Roy Bennett

*Song sounds one octave higher than written.

Wonderful Christmastime

Words and Music by Paul McCartney

*Song sounds one octave higher than written.

THE HAL LEONARD HARMONICA METHOD AND SONGBOOKS

THE METHOD

THE HAL LEONARD COMPLETE HARMONICA METHOD – CHROMATIC HARMONICA

by Bobby Joe Holman

The only harmonica method to present the chromatic harmonica in 14 scales and modes in all 12 keys! This book/CD pack will take beginners from the basics on through to the most advanced techniques available for the contemporary harmonica player. Each section contains appropriate songs and exercises (which are demonstrated on the CD) that enable the player to quickly learn the various concepts presented. Every aspect of this versatile musical instrument is explored and explained in easy-to-understand detail with illustrations. The musical styles covered include traditional, blues, pop and rock.

_____00841286 Book/CD Pack $12.95

THE HAL LEONARD COMPLETE HARMONICA METHOD – DIATONIC HARMONICA

by Bobby Joe Holman

The only harmonica method specific to the diatonic harmonica, covering all six positions. This book/CD pack contains over 20 songs and musical examples that take beginners from the basics on through to the most advanced techniques available for the contemporary harmonica player. Each section contains appropriate songs and exercises (which are demonstrated on the CD) that enable the player to quickly learn the various concepts presented. Every aspect of this versatile musical instrument is explored and explained in easy-to-understand detail with illustrations. The musical styles covered include traditional, blues, pop and rock.

_____00841285 Book/CD Pack $12.95

Prices, contents and availability
subject to change without notice.

THE SONGBOOKS

The Hal Leonard Harmonica Songbook series offers a wide variety of music especially tailored to the two-volume Hal Leonard Harmonica Method, but can be played by all harmonica players, diatonic and chromatic alike. All books include study and performance notes, and a guide to harmonica tablature. From classical themes to Christmas music, rock and roll to Broadway, there's something for everyone!

BROADWAY SONGS FOR HARMONICA
INCLUDES TAB

arranged by Bobby Joe Holman

19 show-stopping Broadway tunes for the harmonica. Songs include: Ain't Misbehavin' • Bali Ha'i • Camelot • Climb Ev'ry Mountain • Do-Re-Mi • Edelweiss • Give My Regards to Broadway • Hello, Dolly! • I've Grown Accustomed to Her Face • The Impossible Dream (The Quest) • Memory • Oklahoma • People • and more.

_____00820009 ....$8.95

CHRISTMAS CAROLS & HYMNS FOR HARMONICA
INCLUDES TAB

arranged by Bobby Joe Holman

This book features 19 holiday songs for diatonic and chromatic harmonicas: Auld Lang Syne • Away in a Manger • Deck the Hall • The First Noel • Jingle Bells • Joy to the World • O Little Town of Bethlehem • Silent Night • What Child Is This? • more. Includes study and performance notes, and a guide to harmonica tablature.

_____00820008 ....$8.95

CLASSICAL FAVORITES FOR HARMONICA
INCLUDES TAB

arranged by Bobby Joe Holman

18 famous classical melodies and themes, arranged for diatonic and chromatic players. Includes: By the Beautiful Blue Danube • Clair De Lune • The Flight of the Bumble Bee • Gypsy Rondo • Moonlight Sonata • Surprise Symphony • The Swan (Le Cygne) • Waltz of the Flowers • and more, plus a guide to harmonica tablature.

_____00820006 ....$8.95

MOVIE FAVORITES FOR HARMONICA
INCLUDES TAB

arranged by Bobby Joe Holman

19 songs from the silver screen, arranged for diatonic and chromatic harmonica. Includes: Alfie • Bless the Beasts and Children • Chim Chim Cher-ee • The Entertainer • Georgy Girl • Midnight Cowboy • Moon River • Picnic • Speak Softly, Love • Stormy Weather • Tenderly • Unchained Melody • What a Wonderful World • and more, plus a guide to harmonica tablature.

_____00820014 ....$8.95

POP ROCK FAVORITES FOR HARMONICA
INCLUDES TAB

arranged by Bobby Joe Holman

17 classic hits especially arranged for harmonica (either diatonic or chromatic), including: Abraham, Martin and John • All I Have to Do Is Dream • Blueberry Hill • Daydream • Runaway • Sixteen Candles • Sleepwalk • Something • Stand by Me • Tears on My Pillow • Tell It like It Is • Yakety Yak • and more.

_____00820013 ....$8.95

TV FAVORITES FOR HARMONICA
INCLUDES TAB

arranged by Bobby Joe Holman

21 top tube tunes arranged for diatonic and chromatic harmonica: The Ballad of Davy Crockett • Theme from Beauty and the Beast • Theme from Bewitched • The Brady Bunch • Bubbles in the Wine • Father Knows Best Theme • Hands of Time • Happy Days • The Little House (On the Prairie) • Nadia's Theme • The Odd Couple • Twin Peaks Theme • Theme from The Untouchables • Victory at Sea • William Tell Overture • Wings • and more.

_____00820007 ....$8.95

FOR MORE INFORMATION, SEE YOUR LOCAL MUSIC DEALER,
OR WRITE TO:

HAL•LEONARD®
CORPORATION
7777 W. BLUEMOUND RD. P.O. BOX 13819 MILWAUKEE, WI 53213

Visit Hal Leonard Online at
www.halleonard.com